Copyright ©2011 by Clare Novak
All rights reserved. No part of thi
transmitted in any form or by any means, electronic or mechanical, including, file sharing, printing, photocopying, recording, or by any information storage or retrieval system, without permission in writing from the copyright owner.

EBIT-Duh!™ Finance for the HR Professional Seminar is a highly interactive and fun way to learn the finance principles in this book. Participants will immediately apply financial information to their own work. Participants engage in group dialogue to share examples and best practices for connecting the dots between HR and the bottom line.

Table of Contents:

Acknowledgements

My heartfelt gratitude goes to everyone who contributed on this project; their generosity is greatly appreciated. Their contributions added to the richness of this work.

Interviews, examples and case studies

- ✓ Gary Bender, CFO
- ✓ Gary Sender, Senior Vice President of Finance
- ✓ Jim Baker, SPHR, Sr. Consultant Talent Management with The Manufacturers' Association of South Central PA
- ✓ Rich Cordivari, VP Learning and Development
- ✓ Sardek P. Love, President and Founder Infinity Consulting and Training Solutions
- ✓ Lauri Plante, Sr. Vice Empress of HR Networking
- ✓ Alan Preston, CEO Preston Leadership
- ✓ Dan Sell, PHR Instructor and HR Leader
- ✓ Mark Vandergast, Partner, Sourcing Solutions Corporation
- ✓ Michelle Yoder, HR Specialist

Each contributor had a passion for the numbers and a zeal for getting the message out to the wider HR community. Finance matters to the HR professional.

Each generously shared his or her time to discuss key concepts, how they are used, and how HR people can learn the mission critical financial concepts.

Reading, Insights and Questions

- ✓ Cindy McGeever, Owner, Top-Sales-Jobs.com
- ✓ Ann McNally, Consultant to Business Owners in Finance and HR
- ✓ Ann Tomalavage, P.E., PMP, LEED AP President, Malarkey Consulting, Inc.

It is invaluable to receive clear-eyed feedback from people who read what an author actually writes and sees the missing pieces. Each contributed her perspective which added to the richness of the finished work. Any errors or omissions are entirely mine.

Lori Colasante and Martha Reeves, also members of our business round table, contributed with encouragement and some very necessary prodding to finish the project. This round table group of dynamic women is invaluable to the author's business success. Thank you with all my heart.

Electronic Publishing Insights

Published authors who were very generous with their time and insights into publishing:
- ✓ Ed Callahan
- ✓ Todd Cohen
- ✓ Annmarie Kelly

Inspiration

To Dave, who admits he should have paid more attention in accounting class.

Community

Thanks to the Society for Human Resource Management Chapters for their warm reception of "EBIT-Duh!™ Finance for HR Professionals" at Chapter dinner meetings and conferences. Also, my thanks go to State Councils for the opportunity to present at State Conferences and finally, I am grateful for the opportunity to present at the SHRM National Conference in 2011.

Association for Talent Development (formerly American Society for Training and Development) Chapters and the National Level has been supportive of this message. I'm grateful for the opportunity to have been twice selected to speak for the International Conference and Expo on the topic of finance.

Introduction

Like you, my background is in training and human resources. Like you, I understand that at the end of the day, organizations need to make money to stay in business. The purpose of this book is to connect the dots between what we in human resources and training do and the bottom line need of businesses to make money.

Everyone in a business needs at least a basic understanding of how the business makes money, how it spends money and whether it's more or less financially healthy than last year. Knowing the basics of finance gives us the language to make a case for initiatives that contribute to the financial health of the business.

My own financial awakening came in two phases. First, calculating return on investment for training made great sense. Of course businesses should expect that training dollars spent create a return. At that point, I started my financial education. Later, as an executive coach, I was facilitating an executive round table and realized that the CEOs were using language I didn't understand. "EBITDA" Huh? My self-judgment was that if I did not understand the language, I didn't belong in the room. That started round two of my financial education.

We can all learn the basics of finance. We aren't expected to be experts; we are expected to be financially literate. This book is written with examples and case studies from our world of HR and Training. There are activities for you to engage in to think about your work and its connection to the financial health of your organization. There are simple examples of what may initially seem like complex concepts. Take a deep breath. Relax and have some fun. Really!

Strategic HR: Money Matters

Strategic HR contributes to the bottom line. We:
- ✓ Are business people with an emphasis in HR
- ✓ Align with our company's financial goals
- ✓ Speak finance

Business People First

"Look, when students in the PHR classes talk about having a seat at the table, I tell them, 'You already have a seat. But, it's a seat at the big Thanksgiving table and you're Uncle Louie. You might be weird Uncle Louie muttering in some HR language nobody understands and nobody wants to sit beside you or you could be Uncle Louie who is interesting to talk to. It's your choice'." *Dan Sell, veteran PHR Instructor*

Interesting Uncle Louie

Everyone who has taken the oft dreaded required public speaking class in college knows *the* rule of engagement—know your audience. Strategic HR professionals understand what interests their audience, the C Suite, in HR initiatives. First and foremost, businesses must be profitable. Strategic HR professionals speak profitability. They know how HR initiatives contribute to the bottom line by either increasing profits or decreasing costs.

Our C Suite audience expects us to know enough about finance to speak knowledgeably about our impact on the numbers. Fortunately, they do not expect us to be finance experts. There are CFOs, VPs of Finance and Finance Departments who are there to be the experts. CEOs will often admit that they defer to finance on certain matters AND at the same time do understand trends, what numbers belong in which buckets, and how the buckets affect the overall financial health of the organization. CEOs have shared that it's about understanding the numbers enough to ask the right questions at the right time.

Lauri Plante, SPHR notes that when you are knowledgeable about finance, you are in a position to ask:

- ✓ What does this number mean?
- ✓ Is it typical?
- ✓ What else is happening?
- ✓ If this trend continues, what happens?

Ms. Plante states, "When you understand the business, if you run into the CEO in the elevator, you can ask an intelligent question about the business." Those intelligent business questions make you interesting. They get people to sit up and take notice of what you have to say. Those questions grab your audience's attention and that's ultimately what you want.

Business is about the numbers and it is also about business processes that produce the numbers. CFO Gary Bender recommends HR professionals, ". . . learn business process tools. Can you map the new hire process or performance review process and find obstacles, gaps, breakdowns or broken processes? Business process knowledge is a pretty unique skill. If you as the HR partner can also be the process facilitator, you will get invited to facilitate executive meetings, breakout sessions, etc. With process knowledge, you can be part of the strategic planning and budgeting team." As Bender points out, business process knowledge puts you in the enviable position of facilitating the conversation at the table.

Furthermore, if you think creatively about adding value to your company's bottom line, you can proactively engage the C Suite, especially the CFO, in topics that interest them. We all know that HR is intimately involved with compensation and benefits. We are also well aware that benefits are a major cost to the organization. Of course our CFO would be interested in a conversation about reducing costs. Why wouldn't we more often engage the CFO in those conversations? CFO Gary Bender notes:

> I attend a benefits contemporary topics/leading edge thinker's session twice a year. Usually 200 HR people show up–senior folks–Director or VP level. I am the *ONLY* CFO who attends and the HR attendees are stunned. Why? Benefit costs are huge and out of control and I want to know what smart people are doing. If *I* were the HR person attending, I would inform the CFO that I am going, review the agenda and pick the CFO's brain on topics that apply to him and offer to debrief with him or create an analysis to review with him. If you want to be really aggressive, invite the CFO to go along and use the day to pick his/her brain on the hot topics and then do an analysis to review later.

As Bender suggests, when we seek to be knowledgeable and engage in conversations our audience is interested in, we are valued. We become interesting dinner companions when we:

✓ Understand what everyone else is talking about
✓ Can ask intelligent questions
✓ Offer new information and perspectives

Align With Financial Goals

"When you are able to frame the initiatives you are proposing within the context of the big picture, and connect the dots from that initiative to your organization's strategy – including financial strategy – you'll have a much greater chance getting executive level support. The more you know about goals and objectives, the better you can judge which ideas fit and which do not." Rich Cordivari, VP Learning and Development

The Financial Strategy Connection

Can you state your company's goals, right now, without looking? If you can state those goals, congratulations! If you can't, why not? Knowing the company's goals is step one. Knowing how the money to achieve those goals is made is even more critical. Let's say your company has the goal of doubling sales in the next three years. If the stray thought "I don't impact sales" crossed your mind, let it keep going. You do impact sales. You hire the sales force.

Once you know the company's goal, the next important question is "How will the company double sales?" Gary Sender, Senior Vice President of Finance, with 25 years' experience poses these questions strategic HR partners should ask themselves:

✓ If my company wants to double sales revenues, how will we do that? Raise prices? Introduce 10 new products? If it's through new products, we'll probably need new sales people.

What do they need to know? What kind of skills do they need to have? What are the human costs?

✓ Will we grow enough to have new government regulations kick in? Will we now have enough people to get reduced per person benefit costs? How can finance use this information?

If you were thinking, isn't the question, really "How will the company double sales profitably?" Congratulations! You are ahead of the curve in making the financial strategy connection. If you asked that question, it means you're aware that it's possible to double sales and see profits remain the same — or even drop. There are numerous business strategies for doubling sales, each with its own financial and HR challenges. Businesses can double sales revenues by:

✓ Acquiring another company (or division of a company)
✓ Accessing new markets
✓ Accessing the same markets differently
✓ Developing new products and services
✓ Raising prices

Let's say your company manufactures a product. In the past, the product has been sold exclusively through wholesalers who brand your product with their name and then sell to the consumer. Your company decides to begin selling directly to the consumer as well as continuing to sell to wholesalers. That strategy needs significant HR involvement in these areas:

✓ How will operations be affected? Are we manufacturing a slightly different version of our product so as to avoid direct competition with our wholesalers? Will we need to be running additional lines in the plant? More shifts? Need training on production?
✓ Or, are we taking the exact same products and packaging them differently under our brand? Who is affected by that change?

What will production need to do differently? Who needs to know about that to do their job effectively?

✓ How are we going to sell direct to the consumer? On the web? How will IT be affected? In person sales calls? Who will we need to hire? How many? What skills will they need? Outbound calling? How do we take our call center from order takers to sales people? Or do we hire trained telemarketers? Do we outsource?

✓ Who needs to know and do what and when?

The answers to these questions and HR's strategic response can be the difference between profitable increased sales and a losing battle. When HR's presence is weak or absent, companies can and do make costly mistakes. One mistake companies may make is assuming the current call center staff can magically transform from order takers to sales people. Strategic HR partners will be at the table pointing out that the assumption may not be correct. Further, the HR partner should come to the table prepared with several plans for staffing properly — including the projected costs of each plan. Of course, some help from the finance department in preparing the costs is warranted.

Clearly, the more closely you can link HR strategies to the financial and business strategies of the company, the more likely you are to be funded for the HR strategies. It is our responsibility to connect the dots from HR initiatives to profitability.

Speak Finance

There are as many ways to learn finance as there are Strategic HR Partners. Reading this book is a start and there are many paths to continue your learning. Numerous great suggestions came from the experts interviewed. Each shared his or her learning path. Here are some of their stories.

Lauri Plante shares her path. "At one point in my career, I was on the operations side of the business. I recommend that everyone step out of HR into operations for a couple of years. Being on the operations side of the business raises your awareness of the numbers. It provides on the job training regarding sales, competitive intelligence, market share and customers." Plante adds," If you're in HR and you are invited to operations meetings — go! Contribute, ask questions, and learn who the experts are, so when you have questions you can ask."

Dan Sell said he learned "Primarily by on the job training." He recommends getting out of the office and talking to people. "Take the time to dialogue with Senior Managers and Financial people and pay attention, listen, and ask questions." Rich Cordivari noted that his "path to this position was rather circuitous. While I have a business degree, I learned in a larger part by trial and error. As an executive in a police department, I had to learn about budgets; however, I only saw a budget from one side. After moving into business, I had to learn the supply side of finance. In fact, I was kicked into the pool rather quickly and distinctly remember a question from my CEO at the time about my sales goals for the coming quarter. I had never sold anything in my life, and wasn't quite sure where to start. Fortunately, I had a terrific mentor who helped and explained things well. I later had the opportunity to run a business which added greatly to my financial acumen."

Gary Sender notes, "Attend seminars with fiduciaries and benefit providers. Ask a million questions of current providers. Read benefit newsletters for financial topics. Stay on top of benefit cost articles in the Wall Street Journal and other periodicals (it's not hard to do topic searches anymore). Read strategic and financial articles."

Align yourself with financial people who can explain enough so that you "get it." You don't have to be an expert when you can find a person who is patient about getting the same question for the 2nd or 3rd time. Don't be afraid to ask; financial people love it when you show interest, is the advice of Lauri Plante.

Need to Know

Speaking finance starts with basic financial literacy. We all have that if we've managed our personal finances. Corporate finance is simply a larger, more complex version of personal finance. On a personal level we have income, outgo, some records of both and a measure of how are we doing as compared to goals, or as compared to last year and the year before. We know that when income exceeds expenses, that's good. The opposite is generally painful.

Of course corporate finance is more complex and yet, it is still grounded on the same basic principles of income, expenses, performance tracking and measures of "how are we doing?" Within those four categories, these are the key concepts which are the focus of this book.
Income:

- Revenue
- Gross profit
- Net profit
- Margin

Assets:

- Cash
- Accounts receivable
- Fixed assets

Expenses:
- Expenses
- Cost of sales
- Total cost

Liabilities and Equity:
- Accounts payable
- Debt
- Stock

Tracking the money:
- Budget
- Income statement
- Balance sheet
- Cash flow statement
- Trend data

Measures of profitability/financial effectiveness:
- ROE (Return on Equity)
- ROA (Return on Assets)
- EVA (Economic Value Added)
- EBITDA (Earnings before interest, taxes, depreciation and amortization)
- Time value of money

EBIT-Duh! Finance for the HR Professional is an introduction to corporate financial literacy. It focuses on the HR profession and uses examples relevant to HR's world and includes advice from successful HR professionals. For more in depth knowledge, there are more formal courses of study as well as numerous reputable on-line resources for further learning.

Think Strategically

It's easy to see the expense side of the Human Resource equation. Wages and benefits are always among the largest expenditures in every organization. It's impossible to ignore all the articles on the cost of health care benefits. However, wages and healthcare costs are the tip of the expense iceberg. There are retirement program costs, training costs, overtime, paid time off, temporary help, benefits administration costs, lost time costs, hiring costs — and the list goes on.

Less obvious on the human cost side is the cost of the space allocated to each person, and the utilities to run that space. There is the cost of the equipment each person uses. There is insurance, the cost of which is based on the company's history of safety. There are perks — company cars, mileage reimbursement for use of personal car and most importantly — caffeine* — in whatever form your employees prefer to ingest it.

*Ok, caffeine may be a breakeven item and maybe even on the income side if it generates productivity

Somewhat less obvious is the income side of the Human Resource equation. It's there, though it may take a bit more financial savvy and work to make the case. HR initiatives that raise productivity (above the cost of the initiative) are on the income side. Making a financial case that an HR initiative will have a positive return on the investment can be done.

Strategic thinking also means looking further down the road than this quarter or this year. Knowing long term trends can position the company to better take advantage and/or to deflect harmful consequences. Think of it this way. You're driving down the road and about a mile up ahead, you see stopped traffic. You have plenty of time to brake slowly and safely. You have time to look in your rear view mirror to see if the person behind you is paying attention and to adjust accordingly. However, if you come around a blind corner and the stopped traffic is mere feet in front of you — you'd best have great brakes, incredible reflexes and a whole lot of luck.

HR professionals who are aware of long term trends add value to the organization. Who will your workforce be in 5, 10, 15 years? How will the increase in obesity in the US affect your healthcare costs in 5, 10, 15 years? How will the mediocre performance of US schools affect your employee pool in 5, 10, 15 years? How will connectivity affect productivity in 5, 10, 15 years? Are you thinking, "Whew, thank heaven I'll be retiring in 5 years? Or, OMG there'll be nothing left for me?
 HR professionals who see trends and are unafraid to challenge conventional wisdom with hard data are "Interesting Uncle Louie."

Additional Resources

- http://www.answers.com
- http://www.investopedia.com
- For regional economic trends, the Federal Reserve Bank has a speaker's bureau
- *Basic Financial Management* Martin, Petty, Keown, Scott
- *Naked Finance* David Meckin
- *The Essentials of Finance and Budgeting*, Harvard Business School Press
- *The Portable MBA in Finance and Accounting* John Leslie Livingstone
- *Thinking Finance* Joel G. Siegel and Shim, Jae K.

Chapter 2: Income and Assets

Making money:
- ✓ Revenue
- ✓ Gross profit
- ✓ Net profit
- ✓ Margin
- ✓ Assets

Revenue

"Revenue is how the company makes money. HR people need to know what business the company is in and it's surprising how many people don't know. Once you know how the company makes money, it's important to know the company's market share and how the company competes, how it sells, what its competitive advantage is." Lauri Plante

Revenue is simply the money that comes into the company. It is also called gross income. Gross income is also referred to as the top line number — the incoming money with nothing subtracted that is quite literally at the top of financial statements.

A simple concept at the heart of things and yet, it is not always as simple as it seems. For example, let's say you've joined PrintPro, an online printing business. If I were to ask you what business PrintPro is in, you might look at me as if I'd gone simple and answer, "Duh, printing." But are you sure you're in the printing business? Before you answer, go have a look at the company's financials. You might find that shipping and handling is a bigger revenue stream than printing. If it is, you're in the shipping and handling business.

If asked, many people would assume that big box warehouse stores are in the bulk products business. They're not. They're in the membership business as it's the memberships that push these stores into profitability, not the very small (if any) profit made on goods sold. There are many examples illustrating that the business the company appears to be in is not the top revenue producer. Some software companies make more money on training than on the software. Some educational institutions are in the grant writing business.

Regardless of the business your organization is in, there is one indisputable rule:
- **Make more money then you spend**

That is the only way to stay in business. Many start-up businesses go out of business because they violate the indisputable rule. Even not-for-profit organizations can have surplus funds to be used for further development or a "rainy day" when fundraising isn't working so well.

Investigative Assignment

If you have even the tiniest question in your mind about what business your organization is in, ask around to determine:

- Who does know?
- How many people are clear about it?
- Do the people on the front line know?
- How would it change their behavior if they did?
- How can HR raise the awareness and contribute to the behaviors that drive revenue?

Mistaken Identity

You've figured out that knowing what business the company is in is crucial to being strategic. Given the above examples, you've most likely figured out that knowing just revenue doesn't tell much about the financial health of the company. Revenues can be rising, flat or falling and at the same time the business can be either profitable or unprofitable. In the recent auto manufacturer bail out, after restructuring, GM saw lower revenue and increased profit.

Key Points:

- ✓ Increased revenue does not automatically mean increased profit
- ✓ Decreased revenue does not automatically mean decreased profit

This may seem obvious to you; however, it may not be obvious to every employee in the company. Questions and comments like these indicate revenue-profit confusion:

- We made $10 million more than last year. Why is my health insurance co-pay going up?
- We're a $600 million company and I didn't get any profit sharing. I'll bet the executives kept it all for themselves.

HR can contribute to employee engagement when we make the difference between revenue and profit clear. Confused employees may feel put upon or worse, cheated. Both conditions lower engagement.

Revenue Trend Data

What is somewhat more helpful in judging the company's financial health is revenue trend data, particularly trend data for the various revenue streams. Fictitious software company Abacus, Inc., has three primary revenue streams: software, customer training, and change management consulting. Here is the revenue trend data.

	Software	Training	Consulting		Total
Current year	$120 M	$4 M	$15 M		$139 M
Previous	$110 M	$5 M	$12 M		$127 M
Previous -1	$100 M	$5 M	$8 M		$113 M
Previous -2	$100 M	$10 M	$8 M		$118 M
Previous -3	$150 M	$20 M	$10 M		$180 M
Total	$580 M	$49 M	$53 M		$682 M

At first blush it looks as if Software and Consulting are recovering nicely from the economic slump. It also looks as if Training is not recovering as well. Being content with first blush could cause us to miss strategic interventions.

Strategic Investigation (Answers P102)

The most strategic thing we can do with those trend numbers is ask questions. Take a moment to look again at the numbers. What questions would you ask about each of the three revenue streams to discover whether HR has a strategic contribution to make?

1. _____
2. _____
3. _____

The answers to your questions will determine HR's strategic involvement. Let's concentrate on the declining revenue from Training. A key question is, "What is the root cause of declining training revenues?" Is it:

- Ineffective leadership?
- Easier, more user friendly software?

- A critical mass of people who know your software well and do freelance training?
- Customers purchasing less training and hoping to get by?
- Training department doing more online and web based training?

Each of those potential root causes dictates a different course of action. Ineffective leadership may require HR stepping in to provide development such as feedback and coaching. If the situation is dire, recruiting a new leader may be in order. Easier software may mean fewer trainers; HR should be planning the attrition. Online and web based training may indicate that the training department may need to staff differently.

Knowing the root cause of changing revenue trends gives HR the ability to analyze and present management with a plan to fix problems, support growth and anticipate future needs based on revenue decline and growth.

Key Points:

- ✓ The root cause of changes to revenue trends, whether up or down, may be an opportunity for HR to make a strategic contribution
- ✓ Proactively seeking the root causes and developing a potential solution adds value to the business

Gross Profit

"Gross" in the finance world refers to a first, rough cut at numbers. "Net" refers to numbers that have been refined, generally by subtracting out a number of specific costs. The easy analogy is a paycheck. Salary is revenue; take home pay is gross profit. This is an imperfect analogy as taxes are deducted from take home pay; think of the tax deducted from a paycheck as "cost of working" and the analogy is a better fit. In business, gross profit is revenues minus cost of goods sold.

Revenues	$200,000
Cost of Goods	-$150,000
Gross Profit	$ 50,000

Like revenue, gross profit alone says little about the financial health of the business. Also like revenue, trends in gross profit are more informative than knowing a single gross profit number.

Net Profit or Net Income

Staying with the easy analogy of the family paycheck, net profit is what's left after necessary expenses are paid. Here are two families and their methods of calculating "net profit" although they are more likely to refer to it as discretionary income. That is, income they can choose to spend or save.

	Family A	Family B
Monthly take home	$5,000	$5,000
Mortgage	$2,000	$2,000
Heat	$ 150	$ 150
Electric	$ 50	$ 50
Water	$ 35	$ 35
Food	$ 250	$ 250
Telephone	$ 80	$ 80
TV	$ 150	
Internet	See TV	
Day care	$1,000	$1,000
Total Expenses	$3,615	$3,465
Net Income	$1,385	$1,535
TV		$ 30
Internet		$ 40

It's clear from a quick look that families A and B view TV and Internet differently. Family A sees them as necessary expenses and Family B sees them as discretionary. That means Family B only buys internet and TV IF there is enough money left over. Both families see mortgage, heat, electricity, etc. as necessary expenses.

Like our two families, "costs of doing business" differ a bit from business to business. Net income in a business is calculated by taking revenues and adjusting for the costs of doing business such as depreciation, interest, taxes, the cost of sales, and any other expenses that the company incurred during the period. This information is found on an Income Statement (See Chapter 4: Tracking the Money). Net income is the bottom line, literally, on the Income Statement.

Like any other number, having trend data is more useful than the single, snapshot number. Knowing this quarter's net income is nice and not terribly informative. Knowing that this quarter's net income is up from last quarter is good. Knowing this quarter's net income and how it compares to the past 8, 12, 16 quarters is better.

	Q1	Q2	Q3	Q4(1 year ago)	Q5	Q6	Q7	Current
Net Income	$22.7	$23	$23.6	$24.9	$22	$22.7	$23	$23.2

- This quarter's net income is $23.2 million. So what?
- This quarter's net income is $23.2 million up from $23 million last quarter. Good and don't celebrate yet
- The past 8 quarters, hum. This quarter is the best this year and it's still down from last year.
- And by the way, our business seems cyclical. Net income is lowest in the first quarter and increases over the year. We're not in an obviously seasonal business, so why are we cyclical?

You've astutely noticed that the best is yet to come. Calculating a rolling average over each quarter is best. Comparing to a rolling average:

- Evens out cyclical trends for seasonal businesses
- Provides a trend over time
- Increases the likelihood of better long term strategic planning and execution

The chart below graphs the same 8 quarters and the above example and adds the rolling average.

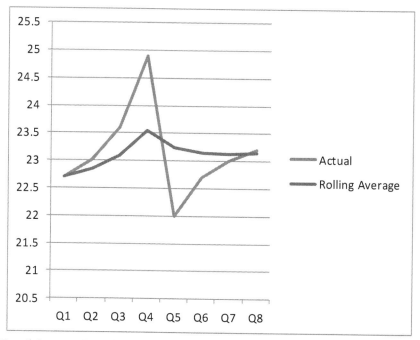

Looking at Q4 alone would probably have resulted in premature celebration. Looking at Q5 compared to Q4 might have caused a spike in healthcare use — for heart and stomach medications. The rolling average demonstrates that there is little cause for either. The rolling average is cause to ask:

- The average has flattened, are we ok with that?
  - o Yes, we have held the line while the majority of businesses in our industry have declined
- If not, what are we going to do about it?
  - o There are numerous potential responses. HR is likely to have a strategic contribution to many of the potential responses.

While quarters are used to demonstrate the principle, monthly rolling averages are frequently used.

HR can impact the bottom line

Companies that have flat lined or worse, declined, in their rolling average net income have to cut costs and/or increase revenues. How they will do that is where HR can make a strategic contribution. HR's contribution to cost cutting:

- Alternative staffing such as contract workers, temps, part timers
- Reducing healthcare costs such as increasing worker contributions, negotiating a new contract with a different provider
- Eliminating positions that don't add value to the company's future
- Work from home to reduce office space rentals
- Reduce training costs through webinars
- Insure that process improvement tools and training are used to reduce costs in other areas

HR's contribution to increasing revenue can include:

- Better staffing in sales and marketing
- Training sales to get every ounce of productivity from those spiffy communication devices
- Coaching sales staff: are they good closers? Do they close profitable sales?
- 80/20 customer analysis: who are the 20% of customers who account for 80% of our revenue? Are we giving them service that reflects their importance? Are we staffed and trained to provide that service?
- *Effective* rewards programs (can you prove it?)
- Instituting a sales culture in the company
- Process improvement in the billing department and the collections area—getting money in the door faster
- Do we have the right people writing contracts? Do they have the skills to negotiate well?

These lists are not exhaustive; however they do give starting points for HR's contribution toward an improving trend line.

Strategic Investigation (Answers P103)

Take a look at your company's Income Statement, then have a conversation with your friendly, local finance person. What questions will you ask to better understand net income and determine HR's impact on it?

1. _____
2. _____
3. _____
4. _____
5. _____

The information you learn will help you better understand how HR's departmental budget fits into the overall corporate finances. When developing your departmental budget, one thing you will most certainly want to be clear on is which HR expenses are "necessary expenses" deducted from gross profit and which are discretionary expenses that will be funded only after net profit is calculated. For example, is that new HRIS system a necessary expense budgeted to be deducted from gross profit? Or is it budgeted only if there is enough left over after necessary expenses are paid?

Remember every department/division is fighting to have its projects and initiatives funded as well. It all comes out of the same checkbook and not everyone gets everything they want. If the new HRIS system is critical to the wellbeing of the company, making that case financially is more likely to win the funding.

A new HRIS system will increase productivity. Fine, so will new computers in operations. So will the spiffiest new communication devices in sales. So will Kaizen training. And so on and so on. The HRIS system will increase productivity, by how many hours a month? At what hourly rate? For how long? Once the "income" numbers are identified, it's also necessary to subtract the expenses. How much will the system cost? Will there be training costs? How much productivity will be lost during the change over from the old system? Only after running the numbers will it be clear whether the system is worthy of funding. If it is worthy of funding, and there are limited funds, is it MORE worthy than the other initiatives?

Quick Tool

In business, time is money. People's time is paid time and therefore saved time is saved money. A quick calculation for converting time to money is:

Loaded hourly rate X hours saved in a given time period X number of periods = Dollars Saved

Loaded hourly rate means salary plus benefits. A conversation with finance is in order to determine which benefits they add in to calculate the loaded hourly rate. Once you have determined what constitutes loaded rates then it is generally acceptable to use an average loaded rate for the people affected by an initiative rather than determining it for each affected person.

Using this tool overcomes some obstacles in calculating return on investment. HR Professionals sometimes express frustration. They would love to calculate the ROI for an initiative such as a wellness program. However, that program covers numerous salary grades, locations, benefits packages, etc. which is information that is not accessible to the HR Professional. By taking aggregate salary and benefits numbers and dividing by the number of people, the resulting hourly rate is "close enough" to demonstrate return. Simply be transparent about the process used to arrive at your numbers.

Mini Case

Everybody in production at PrintPro has been griping about meetings. They take too long; nothing gets done. Nobody follows up; they're a complete waste of time. Time to introduce some process improvement to production meetings and you've done this before so you know you can handle the training internally.

Your back of the envelope cost cutting calculation:
- Annual salary budget for production: $600,000
- Annual benefits budget for production: $240,000
- Number of people in production: 10
- Loaded annual salary: $84,000
- Loaded hourly rate (based on 2,000 hours): $ 42

	Cost of Meeting: Current	Cost of Meeting: Post Training	Savings	Minus Cost of Training	Annual Cost Savings
# People	10	10		11 (trainer incl.)	
# Hrs./week	3	1.5		8 training 8 trainer prep	
Loaded hourly rate	$42	$42		$42	
Materials				$110	
Weeks /year	50	50		1	
Total Annual Cost	$63,000	$31,500	**$31,500**	$4,142	**$27,358**

Congratulations you've just added $27,358 to the bottom line. There are, of course, more sophisticated methods than the back of an envelope. Back of the envelope is good enough to let you know whether an initiative has enough potential return to move forward.

Margin

Margin is gross operating profit divided by sales:

$50,000/$200,000 = 25%

All right, is that a good margin or a bad margin? It depends. Judging a margin as good or bad is industry dependent. In some industries, such as food markets, 1% is a good margin as profit is made primarily on volume of sales. That is, selling a lot of items with only a small margin on each item. Luxury items are the exact opposite. The margin on a 75 karat diamond and emerald necklace is very high. So, as they say, "You only need to sell one."

Knowing your margin as compared to similar companies in your industry is useful as an indicator whether your company is operating more or less profitably. If your industry runs on an average of a 20% margin, your company's 25% margin is great. If the industry runs around 30%, you're lagging behind. In either case, though especially in the lagging case, it's worth investigating to see what initiatives HR can undertake to make a positive impact on profit margins.

Operating Margin is different from Margin/Gross Margin. Operating Margin is a ratio used to measure a company's pricing strategy and operating efficiency. Use which ever measure your company uses. Learn why that particular measure for margin was chosen and why.

$$\text{Operating Margin} = \frac{\text{Operating Income}}{\text{Net Sales}}$$

Mistaken Identity

Employees in retail may confuse mark up and margin. Mark up is the percentage increase a store adds to the price consumers pay over what the store paid. A suit comes in from the manufacturer tagged at $59.99. The store tickets the item at $119.98. This is a 100% markup and why retailers can offer 50% off and stay in business. The margin is a different beast as it subtracts out all the costs accounted for in calculating gross profit. At full price the margin on the suit may be 10% and at markdown may be 5%.

Retailers track the overall margins based on the total sales of full price and markdown items. It's necessary to track that in order to both have sales to attract customers and still be profitable.

Assets

"Assets" is a familiar term. Most of us can name one or two personal assets — in addition to our sparkling personalities and keen intelligence. House and car are two common assets. These are good examples in that they represent an appreciating and a depreciating asset. The housing market, with the exception of a occasional crash, generally appreciates over time. Historically, new homes appreciated by about 5% a year for several decades. Cars depreciate. The second you drive them off the lot they're worth less than you paid. (Caveat: Your state may have a law giving you 48 hours or so to return large purchases at full price). Business assets work the same way. Some appreciate, such as real estate or a nice gold mine that the company owns but isn't mining at the moment. Others depreciate, such as equipment or the corporate jet.

Assets are the "stuff" the company owns and what the stuff is worth. Of course, nothing remains quite that simple. "Stuff" comes in categories — tangible and intangible.

- Tangible assets can include: cash, property, buildings, equipment, things that are physical in nature
- Intangible assets can include: brand names, customer goodwill, copyrights, patents, intellectual property. These are often more difficult attach a dollar amount to and yet, they can be critical to a company's long term viability

A second view of assets comes from how quickly the asset can be converted into cash. Current assets can be easily converted into cash. Current assets can include:

- Cash in bank accounts
- Accounts receivable—money owed the company and due for payment in less than a year
- Inventory

Non-Current assets are assets that are not turned into cash easily and are expected to have a life span longer than a year. Non-current assets can be tangible or intangible. To make things even a little trickier, Capital Expenditure (which sounds like an expense) is really an investment in assets.

Capital Expenditure (CAPEX) Funds are used by a company to acquire or upgrade physical assets such as property, industrial buildings or equipment. This type of outlay is made by companies to maintain or increase the scope of their operations. These expenditures can include everything from repairing a roof to building a brand new factory. In terms of accounting, an expense is considered to be a capital expenditure when the asset is a newly purchased capital asset, such as a building, or an investment that improves the useful life of an existing capital asset, such as adding a new wing to the existing building.

- Newly purchased or improved asset: needs to be capitalized; that is, spread the cost of the expenditure over the useful life of the asset.
- Expense that maintains the asset at its current condition is deducted fully in the year of the expense.
- Services are capitalized when used to build an asset. Internal and external people used to build out an IT system or other capital asset can be capitalized.

In Chapter 5, Measures of Profitability, assets will reappear in the calculation of ROA, return on assets.

Strategic Investigation (Answers P. 104)

HR may not have a great deal of impact on tangible assets and yet, HR can have a profound impact on intangible assets. List the ways you impact intangible assets:

1. _____
2. _____
3. _____
4. _____
5. _____

How does your "C Suite" know you have that impact? What evidence do they see?

1. _____

2. _____

3. _____

4. _____

5. _____

It's vital that HR's contribution to intangible assets be clear and recognized. If you were able to easily identify contributions but unable to cite the evidence, there is room for improvement. Consider how you can identify and position the evidence that HR has a positive impact.

Chapter 3: Expenses and Liabilities

Spending money:
- ✓ Expenses
- ✓ Cost of sales
- ✓ Total Cost
- ✓ Liabilities

Expenses

Understanding what your company considers "costs of doing business" is important to be a strategic player. Companies can and do look at cutting costs to increase profitability. HR has a strategic role to play in anticipating and proactively controlling cost increases and/or cutting costs in such areas as wages, healthcare costs, 401k, payroll, training, etc. Everything that costs money is an expense.

Using the checkbook (a rapidly obsolescent) analogy, income is money going in; expense is money going out. Reducing expenses is one way to insure a bigger checkbook balance, that is, profit.

Businesses have categories of expenses.
- Cost of Goods Sold (COGS)
- Wages, benefits, incentives
- Research and Development (R&D) Expenses are any expenses incurred in the process of finding or creating new products and services. Like CAPEX, these expenses vary greatly by industry.
- Depreciation and amortization
- Telephony, insurance, rent
- Product components

Cost of Sales aka COGS (Cost of Goods Sold)

Cost of Sales is different from one type of business to another. One obvious distinction is whether the business produces tangible goods or services. When a business produces tangible goods, COGS is the costs that go into creating the products the company sells. The costs included in the measure are those that are directly tied to the production of the products. For example, the COGS for a medical devices corporation would include the material costs for the parts that go into the devices along with the labor costs used to assemble the devices (direct labor cost). The cost of shipping the devices to hospitals and the cost of the sales force used to sell them (indirect labor cost) are expenses that would not be included in COGS.

COGS is expensed as the company sells the goods. A basic way to calculate COGS is to start with the beginning inventory for the period and add the total amount of purchases made during the period then deducting the ending inventory. The medical device company may look like this:

Starting Inventory Value	$6 million
Additional Inventory purchased	$2 million
Ending Inventory Value	$5 million
COGS – (inventory component)	$3 million (6 + 2 – 5)

Where did labor go? The cost of labor includes wages, payroll taxes and benefits for the people directly involved in producing the devices and is a second component of COGS. Devices are priced to account for the cost of components plus the labor to assemble them *and* a profit margin.

Cost of Sale (COS) is a more fitting term for businesses that provide services rather than goods. Cost of Sales is the direct labor costs for the service. Direct labor, in this case, is the wages, payroll taxes and benefits for the people providing the service.

COS or COGS is subtracted from revenue to produce the gross profit number.

Mini Case

PrintPro is experiencing increased pressure to lower its prices. Small consumers are abandoning ship in favor of bigger, cheaper online printing houses. Larger consumers are shopping for volume discounts. PrintPro needs to find ways to lower the Cost of Sales. One way is to increase the cost of shipping and handling, but consumers are pushing back on that cost as well. Since raising prices doesn't seem to be an option, driving cost out of the business is critical.

Operations and Shipping agree that they can be more rigorous in pursuing process improvements. Both departments believe they can reduce expenses by 1-2% in the next 3 months. Everyone breathes a sigh of relief and the meeting ends. Not exactly. Everyone knows that labor is a large cost and looks at the HR Business Partner. Well HR? What's your contribution? Fortunately PrintPro has an astute HR Business Partner who anticipated cost cutting measures. Deidre analyzed lost time costs and found some interesting information. Sick time use is up from last year. People were staying out longer for minor injuries this year. Upon closer examination, Deirdre found that those increases were all people who reported to one supervisor. Deirdre's plan is to spend time out on the floor with that supervisor and her people. By doing so, she hopes to discover and correct the root cause of the increased lost time. Deirdre will bring a detailed cost analysis back to the management team that will include current lost time costs, proposed cost of the intervention and the expected reduction in lost time costs. Deirdre is also investigating more proactively managing return to work after injuries.

Reducing HR Expenses

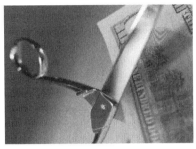

We've all found ways to reduce certain expenses in our personal lives, be it sales, coupons, frequent customer programs or good old fashioned negotiating. Similar tools can be applied to reducing HR expenses in our organizations. By working with our purchasing department, we can leverage existing tools.

Mark Vandergast, Partner, Sourcing Solutions Corporation, shares ways to cut expenses:

- Create a competitive scenario among vendors by talking with the top 3. When a company single sources, it loses leverage.
- Sellers are more motivated negotiate and discount within 60 days of their fiscal year end (or 30 days from quarter end).
- Identify who you buy from already and determine if they will give you a discount for more business. Purchasing Departments should consolidate Master Agreements—rather than have a Master Agreement from every division. A single Master Agreement with a vendor will give you more favorable terms because it clearly defines the amount of business your organization does with that vendor.
- Ideally, 80% of your business should go to 20% of vendors. This allows your organization to leverage buying power AND keep administration manageable AND keep some competition.
- Leverage purchases by other areas of your company. For example, if Operations is purchasing an enterprise wide software system, can you get the vendor to throw in a learning management module for free in order to seal the deal?

Total Costs

Total costs are a detailed analysis of ALL the costs associated with a specific business initiative. For example, clearly the cost for advertising a job opening or paying a recruiter are expenses tied to hiring. The total cost of hiring would include much more: the loaded hourly salary of *everyone's* time who is involved in the hiring process, productivity lost during the vacancy period, lost opportunity costs, etc.

"Total cost, whether it's the cost of sick days, training programs, benefit programs, training (in house or third party) and the appropriate analyses of those costs–long term or short term, expensed or "capitalized" as a long term investment (there are accounting rules that can actually allow capitalization and depreciation over time-it would really impress the CFO if the HR person understood when capitalization of training costs can actually help the current period income statement. I would be stunned). AND THEN put the analysis concepts to use. I can think of many opportunities to use analysis and cost knowledge:

- Cost of recruiting
- Cost of retention
- Cost of layoff, additional overtime
- Use of third party contractors
- Total cost of benefits
- Trends and impacts on single, married, family employee groups
- Cost of 401k and participation trends
- Work comp trends and cost of renewal options
- Consideration of self-insurance for work comp, health or other insurance
- Structuring of employee co-pay, labor cost negotiations or trends, etc.

Find some way to present a monthly topic of interest to top leadership. Give insurance costs and trends ideas. Don't do it three weeks before a huge annual increase. Anticipate, analyze, be proactive, gather inputs, lead brainstorming sessions and use your brokers, advisors and others to do a lot of the analysis and heavy lifting. Ask your advisors to do the analysis that would apply and that their "smartest clients" have them do. Steal best practices-especially those that impress the CEO and CFO, etc." Gary Bender, CFO

In Chapter 2, there was a back of the envelope calculation for an Effective Meetings training program. It was back of the envelope — no more no less. The "Minus cost of training" column in this Back of the Envelope calculation shows only the costs *obviously* associated with training.

Here is the Back of the Envelope with the "cost of training" section highlighted:

	Cost of Meeting : Current	Cost of Meeting : Post training	Savings	*Minus cost of training*	Annual Return
# people	10	10		*11 (trainer incl.)*	
# hrs./week	3	1.5		*8 training 8 trainer prep*	
Loaded salary	$42	$42		*$42*	
Materials				*$110*	
Weeks /year	50	50		*1*	
Total Annual Cost	$63,000	$31,500	**$31,500**	*$4,142*	**$27,358**

Concentrating for the moment on only the cost of training, a Total Costs analysis is much more thorough than the back of the envelope numbers highlighted above. Think of the difference between the quick back of the envelope and the detailed Total Costs this way. You are trying to decide whether to keep your old car or buy a new one. A back of the envelope cost analysis might only include:

- Cost of repairing the old car for the years you keep it vs. new car cost
- Insurance cost increase

Total Costs would ALSO include:

- Loss of interest earned on the money you're saving to put a down payment on a new car (take the money out now vs. leave it in to earn interest for 6 more months)
- Interest paid out on a new car loan

- More expensive parts on the new car, tires for example
- Your time spent at the repair shop with the old car
- Time rearranging kiddie transport when the old car is in the shop
- Anti-stress medications needed with the old car (some companies are actually this detailed in a Total Costs analysis)

Just as you should consider the cost of your own time sitting at the repair shop, Total Costs in business takes into account lost productivity (people aren't producing while they're in training), and overtime costs if people are taken off the line. The table below shows the Total Costs of training for PrintPro's Effective Meetings course:

Costs	Pre Trainir	During	Post training	Total Cost
Salary Time Costs:				
Scheduling 11 people x 10 minutes X $42	$46			
Registration 10 x 5 min. x 42	$35			
Reminders 1 x 20 min x 42	$12		$12	
Pre Work/ Post Work 10 x 30 x 42	$210		$210	
Trainer Prep 8 x 42	$336			
Materials production time 1 x 42 x 2	$84			
Training & Follow up coaching 11 x 8 x 42 11 x 4 x 42		$3,696	$1,848	
Cost of Consumables:				
Manuals	$110			
Food		$250		
Meeting Room Rental		$250		
Mileage		$375		
Lost productivity/opportunity*		$2,225	$1,113	

Total Cost		$833	$6,796	$3,183	$10,81

Lost productivity/lost opportunity costs are very specific to the business, the people who are selected for the training and the time away from work. These costs are best worked out in conjunction with the department(s) affected and finance. For example in an inbound call center, taking 5 people away from the phones for training for one hour results in 10 dropped calls. Each dropped call is worth "X" dollars. "X" is determined by the average order amount and a percentage of lost customer lifetime value as some customers will just go elsewhere when the phone isn't answered in a timely manner.

What will be immediately obvious is that the back of the envelope calculation of training costs is significantly lower than the Total Costs. PrintPro's situation is also fairly straight forward. There are likely to be additional costs in larger, more complex organizations. For example, one large organization has a charge back for utilities (electricity, heat, and water) used in training rooms and the nearby restrooms.

Keep in mind that while Total Costs seem high, a more detailed financial analysis of benefits may also be higher than the back of the envelope calculation. For example, at PrintPro, the back of the envelope calculation of return includes only the time saved by shortening meetings. A more extended calculation can also include the productivity increases that result from effective meeting tools. Those productivity increases could include:

- Rigorous follow up resulting in more goals being met in a timely manner
- Supervisors and managers using the meeting tools in other meetings and saving time in there as well
- Faster problem resolution
- Increased skill levels

At PrintPro, production remains steady when supervisors and managers are in meetings. The lost productivity comes from the trouble shooting for customers and roadblock removal supervisors and managers do. These events are, of course, not evenly spread out day by day. Therefore, PrintPro's HR partner negotiated this number based on the agreement of lost productivity/opportunity as averaged out over a period of time.

Liabilities

Liabilities are simply what the company owes to outside parties, such as loans or accounts payable — what the company owes another company or individual. Liabilities come in two varieties, current and long term.

Current liabilities are debts that need to be paid within a year. PrintPro decides to buy a new, high speed color printing machine net 90. That is a current liability as it needs to be paid for within the 90 day window. To complicate current versus long term liability just a little, the accrued interest payment on a long term loan is a current liability.

Long-term liabilities are debts and other non-debt financial obligations which are due a year or more from the date of the balance sheet on which they are recorded. A 30 year mortgage is an example of a long term liability. The interest on this month's mortgage payment is a current liability.

Debt in business can be incurred to make some purchases and/or to pay expenses, just as individuals incur debt to buy a new flat screen TV or take out a home equity loan to remodel. Borrowing money costs money. Anytime a business can reduce its borrowing, it reduces expenses by the amount of the interest paid out.

There is of course, an exception to the borrowing rule. Businesses may also choose to take on a certain amount of debt to expand, to buy out another company or as leverage. Leverage as a use of debt will be discussed in Chapter 5, Measures of Profitability.

Strategic Investigation (Answers P106)

What does HR do that has a positive impact on the company's liabilities, that is, use of debt?

1. _____

2. _____

3. _____

4. _____

5. _____

If you had difficulty coming up with something, it's time to buy your favorite finance person a cup of coffee or perhaps chat with a more senior HR person in your network. Here's a hint. Think about timing. When money comes in and when it goes out can determine whether a company needs to take on short term debt. HR oversees a lot of big bills. Can you negotiate more favorable payment terms? Discounts if you pay quickly? 45 days instead of 30 for regular payments? A discount for electronic funds transfer? Does starting a group of temps on the 15th instead of the 5th reduce or eliminate borrowing? The larger the organization you work for, the more impact these decisions have on the bottom line. Driving a penny of cost out of a process you do once a day, nets you $3.65 minus weekends and holidays. Driving a penny of cost out of a process you do 100 times a day or 1,000 times a day in the company nets you — well, you figure it out. Don't be afraid of wearing out a calculator.

Chapter 4: Tracking the Money

Tracking the Money:
- ✓ Budget
- ✓ Income Statement
- ✓ Balance Sheet
- ✓ Cash Flow Statement
- ✓ Trend Data

Financial Statements

"It's important to understand the financial statements, top, bottom and everything in between. I liken it to a checkbook. There are the must pay items, like electricity, water, etc. and if you're lucky you have some discretionary money left, that's profit. In business, everything comes out of the same checkbook. Funding an HRIS, a compensation system or a performance system, all come out of the same checkbook as every other expense. You need to be able to justify the investment and make a business case for the expense."   Dan Sell

Budget

Yes, the "b" word. Budgets are the poor, misunderstood planning tools of the financial world. Often times they elicit the other "b" word from people asked to put them together. Rather than cussing the budget process, try to give it a little love and understanding.

A budget is a planning tool that brings all the financial aspects together for coherent, logical commerce. Budgets are in place to help companies meet financial goals. In some ways, this process is no different from a personal or family budget. People who want to meet a particular financial goal, such as to fund a vacation or retirement, often put plans in place to measure how they are progressing toward that goal.

Let's say you've decided to go on your dream vacation and it will cost you $10,000. So far, you haven't put more than a couple hundred dollars away. Rather than give up on your dream, you decide to put yourself on a budget. You decide that you want to go on that vacation in 5 years, no matter what. Based on needing to save $9,800 ($10,000 - $200), your annual savings must be $1960. Since that seems a bit daunting, you break it down to $165 a month. Easier to grasp and still, where will it come from? It will come from same place it comes from in business—increasing income and/or decreasing expenses.

Monthly Budget	Current	New	Savings
Monthly Income	$4,000	$4,000	
Monthly Expenses			
Heat-averaged	$100	$100	
Phone	$85	$45	$40
Internet	$66	$66	
Rent	$1,200	$1,200	
Insurance	$85	$85	
Electric	$45	$45	
Groceries	$120	$120	
Eating Out	$400	$350	$50
Adult beverages	$150	$125	$25
TV	$75	$75	
Gas - auto	$145	$145	
Clothes	$250	$250	
Entertainment	$200	$150	$50
College loan	$500	$500	
Car loan	$450	$450	
Miscellaneous	$129	$129	
Total	$4,000	$3,835	$165

A real budget is interesting as it forces honesty. Where are you spending your money — really? Right now this budget is a lovely table and as long as you stay on budget, you needn't worry about it again. When you get OFF budget is when the budget becomes a useful tool. In what expense category did something change? Why did it change? Is this a temporary change or long term variance?

Your goal was to cut back on eating out by $50 a month and you didn't. Ok, you can fix that by getting back on track next month (by saving $100) or over two months (by saving $75 a month). That was easy. But suppose your insurance goes up by $25 a month. You have two options. One, find a new insurer at the old rate or make cuts in other expenses to make up that $25.

Budgeting in business is basically the same thing as a personal budget on steroids. The budget is there to be used as a tool for reaching goals. When the planned progress toward the goals is on budget, then all's well. When the company goes "off budget" it's time to diagnose why and develop a plan to get back on budget. It's that simple.

And it's not. Of course, organizational budgets are a bit more complex than personal ones, even though they are based on the same principles. First, organizational budgets come in two different packages: operational and capital.

Operational Budget

Operational budgets are generally one year budgets, based on the fiscal year for the particular organization. Remember, the budget is a tool to achieve financial goals. Therefore, the numbers must be realistic. The days of "tack 10% onto last year" are over. There are three ways to build operational budgets:

1. Top down—the executive team sets the high level budget and the divisions/functional areas create budgets aligned with the given numbers
2. Bottom up—Divisions/functional areas develop their budgets which are then merged into creating the operational budget
3. Collaborative—Give and take to reach a negotiated, agreed upon budget

Regardless of the methodology used to create the budget, HR needs to produce realistic numbers, just as any operations manager would. This is the time to wear out your calculator and if necessary, be creative in finding ways to reduce costs. Better yet, anticipate budget needs and develop a plan to hold or reduce costs AND to increase productivity.

Capital Budget

Capital budgeting is the process in which a business determines whether projects such as building a new plant or investing in a long-term venture are worth pursuing. However, because the amount of capital available at any given time for new projects is limited, management needs to use capital budgeting techniques to determine which projects will yield the most return over an applicable period of time.

As an HR professional, you need to know whether the initiatives you're proposing come out of the operational budget or the capital budget. Capital budget items are in competition with one another. The organization should analyze the items and choose those that are projected to produce the greatest return over an allotted time period. The better the financial case HR can make for its initiative, the more likely it is to be funded. For example, an HRIS system may be in the capital budget. If you make your case and the system is funded, buy it during the year it is budgeted as capital budgets are "use 'em or lose 'em."

A Case of Mistaken Identity

A financial forecast is not a budget or vice versa. A financial forecast is the same idea as a weather forecast — frequently revised based on reality. In the winter of 2011, the weather forecasters had two tracks for a particular storm. All of forecasters went with the track that had the storm being a non-event. By the next day the storm had taken the other track (the low probability track) and became an "over performing" storm, dumping over a foot of snow.

A financial forecast is where finance people think the numbers will go based on the economic conditions at the time they make the forecast. As we know, conditions change.

Income Statement*

*The income statement goes by a lot of aliases. Most commonly used are "statement of income," "statement of earnings," "statement of operations," "statement of operating results" or the good old P&L which stands for profit and loss. A rose is a rose is a rose—as long as you're profitable. If you're not, you might want to call it something less savory. The income statement is divided into two parts: the operating and non-operating sections. The portion of the income statement that deals with operating states information about revenues and expenses that are a direct result of the regular business operations. For example, PrintPro's operating items section would talk about the revenues and expenses involved with printing.

The non-operating items section discloses revenue and expense information about activities that are not tied directly to a company's regular operations. For example, if the PrintPro sold a factory and some old equipment, then this information would be in the non-operating items section. PrintPro's Income Statement below shows a comparison of fiscal years 2009 and 2010. Fiscal years may or may not align with calendar years. In order to take advantage of some tax laws, fiscal years can start any month of the calendar year. Once the company specifies the fiscal year, say starting July 1 and ending June 30, they need to stick with it. On any financial statement, if a number is in parentheses, it is outgo, that is, a loss or expense.

Income Statement For PrintPro FY 20xx and 20xy		
	20xx	*20xy*
Net Sales	$1,500,000	$2,000,000
Cost of Sales	($350,000)	($375,000)
Gross Income	$1,150,000	$1,625,000
Operating Expenses	($235,000)	($260,000)
Operating Income	$915,000	$1,365,000
Other Income (Expense)	$40,000	$60,000
Extraordinary Gain (Loss)	-	($15,000)
Interest Expense	($50,000)	($50,000)
Net Profit Before Taxes (Pretax Income)	$905,000	$1,360,000
Taxes	($300,000)	($475,000)
Net Income	$605,000	$885,000

Mini Case (Answers P107)

Based on PrintPro's Income Statements for 20xx and 20xy, what conclusions can you draw about the financial health of the company?

1. _____

2. _____

3. _____

If PrintPro continues the upward trend into the next 2 or 3 years, what can you, the HR Partner anticipate and plan for?

1. _____

2. _____

3. _____

Balance Sheet

A balance sheet is a financial statement that summarizes a company's assets, liabilities and shareholders' equity at a specific point in time. These three balance sheet segments detail what the company owns and owes, as well as the amount invested by the shareholders or owners. The amount invested by shareholders and/or owners is referred to as equity, just as the amount you've already paid on your mortgage plus any appreciation in the property value is homeowner's equity.

 It's called a balance sheet because the two sides (assets and liabilities/equity) balance out. Below is an example of a simple balance sheet for a market. This balance sheet meets the financial criteria of showing assets and liabilities for the current term. This one happens to show year end data. Balance sheets are usually calculated at least quarterly and as often as monthly in larger organizations.

Balance Sheet		Madeline's Market	20xx
Assets		Liabilities	
Current		Current	
Cash/investment	$ 900,000	Accounts Payable	$2,420,000
Receivables	$ 580,000	Short term debt	$ 200,000
Inventories	$3,900,000	Taxes payable	$ 137,000
Prepaid expenses	$ 60,000	Total Current Liabilities	$2,757,000
Total Current Assets	$5,444,000	Long term debt	$ 200,000
Property, plant & equip	$3,800,000	Owner's Equity	$6,283,000
Total Assets	$9,240,000	Total liabilities and Owner's Equity	$9,240,000

Cash Flow Statement

Money flows in; money flows out. A cash flow statement shows cash in and cash out during a specified period of time. In a profitable company, more flows in than flows out. When the reverse happens, the company is in trouble.

An easy way to see cash flow patterns is to picture different kinds of family finances:

- Family A runs its finances frugally and believes in saving for a rainy day. They also avoid debt believing that the only debt they should have is a mortgage—and they wish they didn't have that debt. Assuming that Family A has a reasonable income, they should have a nice, consistent, positive cash flow.
- Family B thinks a little bit of financial risk can have rewards and taking on a bit of debt for car and college is an investment in the future. Assuming that Family B has a reasonable income, makes a decent return on "slightly risky" investments and suffers only occasional, short term setbacks, they too will have a positive cash flow most of the time. They may experience somewhat higher highs and somewhat lower lows than Family A.
- Family C thinks fiscal restraint is for wimps. They make high risk investments in hopes of equally high payoffs. Sometimes that works and sometimes it doesn't. Family C is likely to have erratic cash flow. Excess cash at times and high debt at others.
- Family D lives from paycheck to paycheck. More often than not debt exceeds income. They make minimum payments and hope for the best. They get by on a fragile system that collapses at the first downturn in income. More flows out than in.

Carefully reading Cash Flow Statements will let you know whether you work for company A, B, C or D. In the olden days before deregulation, banks and utilities would be like family A. Most companies are like family B, willing to take some calculated financial risks in order to get some bigger gains. C Companies are more common in good economic, freewheeling times when there is likely to be easy credit and ready growth. D companies do exist, but not forever.

Think of the number of the retailers that turned out to be D companies and went out of business during the recent economic downturn. They did not have the reserves to ride out the bad times. For many years, a number of retailers had poor cash flow during most of the year and hoped for copious holiday spending to make up for it. As they learned, hope is not a strategy.

Shown below is the cash flow statement of a privately held software maintenance company. As you can see, revenues and expenses are both detailed and at the end of the statement is the cash balance of the company. Note that the cash balance for the current month and the year to date are identical. Note also that at some point during the year, the owner needed to put money into the company. What conclusions can you draw about the cash flow situation of the company?

Cash Flow Statement

December 20xx	Current Month	Year to Date
Scheduled Payments	$5,465	$32,860
Operating Revenue:		
Monthly service contracts	$3,335	$18,757
Prepaid service	0	$ 995
Other Income	$81	$ 131
Total operating revenue	$3,406	$29,701
Operating Expense		
Service delivery costs	$450	$2,250
Mailing	$ 2	$ 10
Marketing	$ 555	$ 813
Supplies	$ 313	$ 313
Electricity	$ 75	$ 384
Internet	$ 116	$ 425
Miscellaneous	$ 22	$ 83
Total Operating Expenses	$1,534	$ 4,281
Net Income	$1,871	$15,419
Beginning Cash Balance	$1,448	
Increase (decrease) from Net Income from Operations	$1,871	$15,419
Increase (decrease) from Owner Capital Accounts		
Owner Draw	($2,900)	($16,000)
Owner contribution of Capital	0	$ 1,000
Ending Cash Balance	$ 419	$ 419

Clearly one conclusion is that the owner takes a draw just as one might pay a salary. In a privately owned company, taxation may play a role in what the owner choses to leave in the business and what he or she chooses to draw. This is a private company, note that a corporation would also have to list tax payments.

Strategic Investigation (Answers P108)

Read your company's cash flow statement, in fact read several. Write the questions you have about them that you want to ask your friendly finance person.

1. _____
2. _____
3. _____
4. _____
5. _____

Once you have a good understanding of your company's cash flow, analyze the HR initiatives underway. Which of them has a positive impact on cash flow? Which have a negative impact?

HR Initiatives with a positive influence on Cash Flow	Negative Influence:
1.	1.
2.	2.
3.	3.
4.	4.
5.	5.

Given your company's financial goals, which initiative would have the greatest positive impact on cash flow? Remember that *reducing* a negative impact can have a positive impact on cash flow. The next step is to run some back of the envelope calculations and talk them over with finance. Finance can help you shape the numbers into a more formal proposal to take to leadership.

Mini Case (Answers P109-110)

Let's say you've noticed that the amount paid to contract workers has been on the rise. Contractor expenses are increasing by several thousand dollars every month. Could it be time to hire? Would an adding internal position(s) help cash flow by reducing costs?

As a good HR person, you reach for the antacids when you learn that technical departments have hired back experts that were laid off last year. Yes, they did hire them back through technical consulting firms but at a premium. Legal issues aside (this is a finance book) is this the most cost effective way to get the work done? Investigation reveals the following:

- Contractor expenses are currently $27,000 per month
- $21,000 went to RentATechie.com
- $11,000 is for your own former employee, a maintenance engineer, $7,000 is for your own former electrical engineer, and $3,000 is for a second electrical engineer.

A conversation with the Operations Manager reveals:
- He'd like to hire one person but the CEO said there was a hiring freeze
- To hire just one person, he'd need a new position with new duties and responsibilities

Identify the numbers/financial information you need to make a **financial** case for hiring rather than continuing to contract:

* _____
* _____
* _____
* _____

Trend Data

"Trend data is also important. Is this quarter up or down? How does that compare to last year? Is the trend due to something the company controls or not?" Plante
"Get on the distribution list for the regularly issued finance reports for the group you are supporting. Look at actual against projected and why there is a difference. Understand variances you see on those reports. What happened to make performance better or worse?
Don't glaze over but pick out the message the numbers are trying to communicate. Trending can help you figure out what to adjust in HR levels and compensation. Ask a lot of questions. Pay attention in meetings when the finances are presented." Sender

Trend data is useful because it lets you know if the number you're seeing is a once off or a pattern.

Income Statement For PrintPro			
	20xx	**20xy**	**20xz**
Net Sales	$1,250,000	$1,500,000	$2,000,000
Cost of Sales	($345,000)	($350,000)	($375,000)
Gross Income	$905,000	$1,150,000	$1,625,000
Operating Expenses	($230,000)	($235,000)	($260,000)
Operating Income	$675,000	$915,000	$1,365,000
Other Income (Expense)	$20,000	$40,000	$60,000
Extraordinary Gain (Loss)	-	-	($15,000)
Interest Expense	($50,000)	($50,000)	($50,000)
Net Profit Before Taxes (Pretax Income)	$645,000	$905,000	$1,360,000
Taxes	($240,000)	($300,000)	($475,000)
Net Income	$405,000	$605,000	$885,000

Identify the obvious conclusions you can draw from PrintPro's three years of data: **(Answers P113)**

- _____
- _____
- _____
- _____
- _____

PrintPro's numbers, initially look good. Income numbers are continuously increasing, and it's particularly good that Net Income continues to increase, because that lets us know that expenses, while growing, are not growing disproportionately. Now pull out a calculator. Calculate the following for each year:

- Cost of sales as a percentage of Net Sales each year
- Operating expenses as a percentage of Net Sales each year

	20xx	20xy	20xz
Cost of Sales %			
Operating Expenses %			

What do those numbers tell you about PrintPro's financial health?

- _____
- _____

As an HR Partner, what specific initiatives can you undertake/continue that will have a direct financial impact on continuing those financially healthy trends?

- _____
  _____
- _____

Chapter 5: Measures of Profitability

Measures of Profitability:
- ✓ ROE (Return on Equity)
- ✓ ROA (Return on Assets)
- ✓ EVA (Economic Value Add)
- ✓ EBITDA (Earnings before interest, taxes, depreciation and amortization)
- ✓ Time/value of money

Return on Equity

Return on equity (ROE) measures the rate of return on the ownership interest (shareholders' equity) of the common stock owners. It measures a firm's efficiency at generating profits from every unit of shareholders' equity. ROE shows how well a company uses investment funds to generate earnings growth.

In other words, it is a measure of a corporation's profitability that reveals how much profit a company generates with the money shareholders (or owners, in a private company) invested.

Calculated as:

ROE= Net Income/ Shareholder Equity

The ROE is useful for comparing the profitability of a company to that of other firms in the same industry.
You got this far, don't fuzz out. Let's say you're a parent who is attempting to teach your two teenagers how to generate income. You loan each of them $100 to start a summer business and explain to each of them that you are now a shareholder and expect a return on your $100.

Teenager 1, Dave, buys a used lawn mower and starts a mowing service. Teenager 2, twin sister Daphne, starts a pet sitting business. At the end of the summer, the day of reckoning arrives. The twins each present you with their accounting numbers.

	Dave	Daphne
Gross Income	$4,800	$4,400
Salary	$4,000	$4,000
	$ 500	$ 350
	$ 300	$ 50
Shareholder's equity	$ 100	$ 100
	3 or 300%	.5 or 50%

Based on the numbers (not the kid you like better) which kid should you invest in next summer? Stop being a parent and start being an investor. The answer is not "both" it's "Dave."

Two companies may look similar on paper as well. In the example below, one variable, "liabilities," changes the ROE.

Eat and Get Out		Eat and Get Gas	
Total Assets (TA)	$1,000,000	Total Assets (TA)	1,000,000
Net Income (NI)	$ 200,000	Net Income (NI)	200,000
Liabilities	$ 500,000	Liabilities	250,000
Owner's Equity (OE)	$ 500,000	Owner's Equity (OE)	750,000
ROE = Net Assets/Owner's Equity	200,000/500,000= .4 or 40%		200,000/750,000 = .26 or 26%

By incurring more debt (liability) the company is able to generate a higher ROE. This happens because the owner(s) reduced their equity thus showing a higher return with the same net income.

Strategic Investigation

What are the potential relationships of ROE to compensation throughout the organization? **(Answers P114)**

1. _____

2. _____

3. _____

If your executives are incented for achieving a specific ROE, how can they virtually guarantee themselves the bonus?

1._____

The DuPont Formula, also known as the strategic profit model, is a common way to break down ROE into three important components. Splitting return on equity into three parts makes it easier to understand changes in ROE over time.

ROE = Net Income/sales x Sales/Total Assets x Total Assets/Average Stockholder Equity

Net Income/Sales: If the net income increases, every sale brings in more money, resulting in a higher overall ROE.

Sales/Total Assets: If the asset turnover increases, the firm generates more sales for every unit of assets owned, again resulting in a higher overall ROE.

Total Assets/Average Stockholder Equity:
Finally, increasing financial leverage means that the firm uses more debt financing relative to equity financing. Interest payments to creditors are tax deductible, but dividend payments to shareholders are not. Thus, a higher proportion of debt in the firm's capital structure leads to higher ROE.

Return on Assets

Return on Assets, (ROA) tells you what earnings were generated from invested capital (assets). It is best to compare ROA against a company's previous ROA numbers or the ROA of a similar company. The calculation for ROA is:

ROA = Net Income/Total Assets
- If ABC company has a net income of $1 million and total assets of $5 million, its ROA is 20%;
- If DEF Company has as net income of $1 million and total assets of $10 million, it has an ROA of 10%.

Based on this example, which company is better at converting investment to profit?

Based on this example, the ABC Company is better at converting its investment into profit. When you really think about it, management's most important job is to make wise choices in allocating its resources. Anybody can make a profit by throwing a ton of money at a problem, but very few managers excel at making large profits with little investment.

Return on Net Assets (RONA) (Answers P71)

Not to unduly complicate things, RONA, as a measure of financial health, calculates return based on net assets (remember "net" simply means that some costs are subtracted).

Strategic Investigation:

- Who in your organization would rather receive an incentive based on ROA rather than ROE?

  _____

- Who would prefer ROE?

  _____

"ROA is a good internal management ratio because it measures profit against all of the assets a division uses to make those earnings. Hence, it is a way to evaluate the division's profitability and effectiveness. It's also more appropriate here because division managers seldom get involved in raising money or in deciding the mix between debt and equity," James A. Kristy and Susan Z. Diamond wrote in their book _Finance without Fear._

"One of the cardinal rules in managing business professionals is to hold them accountable for only those activities they control. ROA comes close to doing just that."

Mini Case

A small manufacturing company with a current sales volume of $50,000, average assets of $30,000, and a net income of $6,000 (giving it an ROA of $6,000 / $30,000 or 20 percent) must decide whether to improve its current inventory management system or install a new one.

- Expanding the current system would allow an increase in sales volume to $65,000 and in net income to $7,800, but would also increase average assets to $39,000. (7,800 / 39,000 = 20%)

- o Even though sales would increase, the ROA of this option would be the same – 20 percent.

- On the other hand, installing a new system would increase sales to $70,000 and net profit to $12,250. Because the new system would allow the company to manage its inventory more efficiently, the average assets would increase only to $35,000. (12,250 / 35,000 = 35%)

  - o As a result, the ROA for this option would increase to 35 percent, meaning that the company should choose to install the new system.

Economic Value Added

Economic Value Added (EVA) is a measure of a company's financial performance based on the residual wealth calculated by deducting cost of capital from its operating profit. (Also referred to as "economic profit")

The formula for calculating EVA is as follows:
EVA= Net Operating Profit After Taxes (NOPAT) - (Capital * Cost of Capital)

Mini Case

To understand the difference between EVA and its older cousin, net income, here are two takes on the same company.

Using Net Income:

Clare's House of Crocheting. Clare's earned $100,000 on a capital base of $1 million thanks to big sales of baby blankets. Traditional accounting metrics suggest that Clare is doing a good job. Her company offers a return on capital of 10%.

Clare's has only been operating for a year, and the market for baby blankets still carries significant uncertainty and risk. Debt obligations plus the required return that investors demand for having their money locked up in an early-stage venture add up to an investment cost of capital of 13%.

That means, although Clare's is enjoying accounting profits, the company lost 3% last year for its shareholders.

Using EVA:

Conversely, if Clare's capital is $1 million - including debt and shareholder equity - and the cost of using that capital (interest on debt and the cost of underwriting the equity) is $1.3 million a year, Clare will add economic value for her shareholders only when profits are more than $1.3 million a year. If Clare's earns $2 million, the company's EVA will be $.7 million.

- In other words, EVA charges the company rent for tying up investors' cash to support operations. There is a hidden opportunity cost that goes to investors to compensate them for forfeiting the use of their own cash.

EVA captures this hidden cost of capital that conventional measures ignore.

EBITDA

EBITDA, earnings before interest and tax, depreciation and amortization is the amount of profit earned from a firm's normal core business operations. This value does not include any profit earned from the firm's investments (such as earnings resulting from firms that the company has partial interest in) and the effects of interest and taxes.

EBIT and EBITDA exist in order to make apples and oranges look more alike financially. In the past, most companies were bricks and mortar. As the economy shifted toward service industries, it was difficult for investors to compare the two and make a reasonable investment decision.

EBIT is also known as Operating Profit which is calculated: Operating Profit = Operating Revenue – Operating Expenses

EBITDA subtracts out those two bricks and mortar components, depreciation and amortization.

- Depreciation: a portion of the cost of an asset that is subtracted each year until the asset's value reaches 0. This reflects normal wear and tear.

- Amortization: allocating the cost of long-lived assets, including intangible assets, to periods in which their benefits are derived.

Quick, name a depreciating asset that you own. Most people will blurt out "car." That is correct. A car starts depreciating the second you turn the key and drive it out of the dealer's lot. Some cars depreciate faster than others. This is contrasted with an appreciating asset—something that gains value over time, such as a home (until recently). In ancient times computers were so expensive that a company could depreciate them over time. This is a brief history lesson for readers under 30.

Amortization deals with assets, including goodwill, that have value over a long period of time. Let's say you had the foresight to inherit land in South America that just happens to have large copper deposits. Lucky you, with the current appreciation in copper prices. Clearly, you don't want to take all the value of the mine (and all the taxes) in one year. So you and the government come to an equitable arrangement of the useful life of the mine being 30 years. The government very graciously agrees to collect taxes on your mine for the next 30 years.

One of the most frequently asked questions about EBIT-DA is, "How do you pronounce that?" The answer? "Pronounce it the way your CEO and finance gurus pronounce it. Two common pronunciations are "E-BIT-D-A" and "EBIDA."

Time Value of Money

"This concept focuses on being sure we negotiate contracts to get paid in a timely manner; hopefully no more than 30 days. If you get paid on time, then you may not have to borrow money to run your operation which, of course, costs money paid out in interest on that loan." Cordivari

Net Present Value, (NPV) compares the value of a dollar today to the value of that same dollar in the future, taking inflation and returns into account. If the NPV of a prospective project is positive, it should be accepted. However, if NPV is negative, the project should probably be rejected because cash flows will also be negative.

Mini Case (Answers P116)

Your company wants to buy up "Mom and Pop" competitors—let's say HVAC businesses. Your company would first estimate the future cash flows the "Mom and Pop" business would generate, and then discount those cash flows into one lump-sum present value amount, say $750,000. If the owner of the store was willing to sell his business for less than $750,000, the purchasing company would likely accept the offer as it presents a positive NPV investment. Conversely, if the owner will only sell for $750,000 or more, your company wouldn't buy the small business, as the investment would present a negative NPV at that time and would, therefore, reduce the overall value of the company.

- Why should HR care about NPV?

_____
_____
_____
_____
_____

- How can HR affect NPV?

Money and Timing

When money is used in an organization does make a difference in the profitability for that year. In organizations who use a calendar year as the fiscal year, capital budgets are "use it or lose it" during the last few months of the year. Capital budgets are year by year. The money does not carry over. Remember also that both internal and external staff used to build a capital item can also be capitalized.

While Finance would like to see more even spending throughout the year, what tends to happen is a flurry of year end spending. There are numerous reasons for this, including increased negotiating pressure on vendors who are trying to make their yearend numbers.

Mark Vandergast notes:
> Understand your company's purchase process — approvals, getting new vendor in system, whether deliveries and payments need to occur during a particular time period. Finance may have purchase templates you can use. They can then plug in the numbers and give it back to you with recommendations regarding timing, approvals, etc.

Knowing that vendors tend to negotiate at quarter end and yearend, do sourcing work ahead of time. Work with Purchasing and Accounting to have the paper work ready. Then do the purchase when the vendor is eager to sell

Chapter 6: Financial Health

Vital Signs: Better or Worse?

Below are numbers for the same company during two different years. The third column of numbers shows the percentage of change, up or down, from 2010 to 2011. To test your understanding, put a √ in the +/- Impact column if the change is good for the business. Put an X in that column if the change is bad for the business. Finally, state why the Impact is positive or negative.

Profitability	20xx	20xy	% Change	+/- Impact	Why is it + or -?
Revenue	3,150,000	3,500,000	11.11%		
Gross Profit	910,000	1,050,000	15.38%		
Gross Margin %	28.89	30.00	3.85%		
Operating Exp %	20.76	19.29	-7.11%		
EBIT	256,000	375,001	46.48%		
EBIT Margin %	8.13	10.71	31.84%		
Net Income %	3.67	5.18	41.42%		
Working Capital					
Accounts Receivable	431,506	671,233	55.56%		
Accts. Receivable Days	50	70	40%		
Inventory	908,444	1,033,696	13.79%		
Inventory Days	148.03	154	.03%		
Accounts Payable	429,000	402,855	-6.09%		

Profitability	20xx	20xy	% Change	+/- Impact	Why is it + or -?
Revenue	3,150,000	3,500,000	11.11%	√	Demonstrates increase in sales
Gross Profit	910,000	1,050,000	15.38%	√	Sales are more profitable
Gross Margin %	28.89	30.00	3.85%	√	Making more revenue per sale
Operating Exp %	20.76	19.29	-7.11%	√	Operating more efficiently
EBIT	256,000	375,001	46.48%	√	Stronger earnings
EBIT Margin	8.13	10.71	31.84%	√	Higher earnings margin
Net Income %	3.67	5.18	41.42%	√	More profitable at the end of the day
Working Capital					
Accounts Receivable	431,506	671,233	55.56%	X	Customers owe money which could be lost through default. May have to do more short

					term borrowing to cover expenses
Accounts Receivable Days	50	70	40%	X	Customers are paying much more slowly which could cause cash flow issues.
Inventory	908,444	1,033,696	13.79%	X	More inventory
Inventory Days	148.03	154	.03%	X	Sitting around longer
Accounts Payable	429,000	402,855	-6.09%	X	

So, how is the company doing overall? Clearly there is a mix of positive and negative signs.

Strategic Investigation

What do the positive items tell us about the company's financial health now?

1. _____
   _____
2. _____
   _____
3. _____
   _____

What do the negative items tell us to watch out for? What could happen if the negative items persist or get worse?

1. _____
   _____

2. _____
   _____

3. _____
   _____

List the strategic questions you can ask to determine where HR can contribute to the bottom line.

1. _____
   _____

2. _____
   _____

3. _____
   _____

Case Studies

The case studies in this section are actual cases. However, details have been fictionalized to protect the confidentiality of the organization's data. Although fictionalized, the numbers are reflective of the actual situations. Percentages have been kept proportional, that is, in alignment with the actual percentages.

90% Annual Staff Turnover

Chances are when you read "90% Annual Turnover" several thoughts went through your head. If that turnover rate isn't normal in your industry, "yikes" was probably one of those thoughts. After 5 Chapters of a book on finance, with luck, another thought was, "I wonder how much money that is costing us?" If you weren't thinking that, please do so now.

Senior Leadership looked at you and said, "Fix it." For turnover to have Senior Leadership's attention, it's probably causing significant problems in the business metrics. Turnover gets onto upper management's radar screen when it has an adverse effect on the financial metrics of the organization.

Level of Leadership	Financial Focus	Time Horizon
Senior Leadership	Contribution Margins Earnings Ratios Profit / Loss Return on Assets (and those of Mid-Level Management)	3 -5 years
Mid-level Leadership	Cost of Goods Sold Gross Margins Earnings	1 – 3 years
Frontline Leadership	Cycle Times Quality Production Sales	1 year or less

"How to Create and Maintain Effective Business Plans for T&D Programs" by Sardèk P. Love Used with permission of the author

For turnover to be noticed by Senior Leadership, it is likely having an adverse impact on quality, production and cycle times. That in turn has adverse effects on margins which then adversely affect profitability. As a savvy business partner, you will want to do several things:

1. Investigate the root cause of the turnover
2. Identify the specific business metrics affected
3. Identify the target metrics for the business unit

4. Determine cost effective initiatives to meet the business metrics

This organization is a medical insurance provider. The unit within the organization is the underwriting team for individual policies. The team consists of customer service for individual policies, senior underwriters and underwriters and the administrative support for the team. The high turnover rate is among the underwriters, about 25 people, half of whom are senior underwriters. Investigation showed that people would stay the mandatory year in the position and then post internally to transfer out of the department as soon as possible.

As it turns out, underwriting was caught in a vicious cycle. Some of the causes of turnover included:

1. 1 year to underwriting proficiency
2. Salary less than in the claims department
3. Long hours due to not being properly staffed
4. Leadership gap — turf wars, expected weekend work, unwilling to staff appropriately

The high turnover rate virtually guaranteed that people would have to work long hours to keep production rates up and the long hours at a lower rate of pay virtually guaranteed people would leave the team.

After determining the causes of turnover, it was important to identify the target metrics for the team and their current performance against those metrics.

Target Metric	Current Performance	Business Impact	Financial Impact
Less than 5% Error Rate	16% Error Rate	Higher claims payouts Higher insurance fraud rates	Reduced profitability
Less than 21 days cycle time	28-42 days cycle time	Lost sales	$4,500 in revenue per customer lost
12 Applications per Day	7-8 Applications per day	Reduced business	ditto

Both the financial and human impact of those performance levels was significant. The human impact was clearly expressed in the turnover rate. In the insurance industry, a regulated industry, insurers are required to tell the State expected financial numbers each year. Those numbers included the % of revenues in reserves, % for claims, and % per admin costs. After subtracting those numbers, profit was in the 3-5% range. The financial impact was reduced profit.

Production

Like most situations, a single initiative would not cure the problems and miraculously produce the expected metrics. The end goal was straightforward though. Raise throughput and lower errors. Much like triage in nursing, the first thing was to staunch the bleeding — with an emergency rescue team. The rescue team of trained personnel would go in and help underwriting when they got too overwhelmed. Just getting some help slightly reduced the error rate as people weren't rushing quite so much.

An emergency rescue team is just that — emergency rescue and not a long term solution. A long term solution to productivity was to bring new hires up to speed faster. It was taking a full year to bring people to full proficiency — and then they'd leave. New hire training was reevaluated and short term production and efficiency rates were set for each quarter during the first year on the job.

1 - 3 Months	Process 2-4 apps / day	Accuracy of 65% - 75%
4 - 6 Months	Process 4 - 6 apps / day	Accuracy 70% - 80%
7 - 9 Months	Process 6 - 8 apps / day	Accuracy 80% - 95%

The training team was able to conservatively quantify and reaffirm the production and quality results once training was completed. Based on those metrics, Operations could make more accurate budget projections, thereby preventing negative budget variances throughout the year

Error Rate

In this case, errors made by the underwriters happened when they overrode the system decision and gave premium insurance to high risk persons. This is costly to the company in that the person's medical risk outweighed the premiums being charged. In addition, a small percentage of the people approved in this way applied for insurance with the intent to commit fraud. A small number of these cases were caught when the person submitted for back or neurological issues within the initial 30 days of the contract. As the fraud department was relatively small, few of the people committing fraud were caught. Fraud results in lost revenues.

The Quality staff was brought into the picture to monitor error rates. As we know, simply paying attention to something, be it error rates, productivity or morale produces a change. Once the underwriters were aware that error rates were monitored, those error rates fell from 16% to 12%.

The Quality Staff analyzed the error rate data and found that new trainees had higher quality work than senior people. This being a real case study, supervisors challenged the data saying that it couldn't possibly be correct. It was. As it turns out, once a person completed initial training to become an underwriter, no further training occurred. The solution was highly focused training for the Senior Underwriters on the top 7 issues that they identified.

Over a period of two years, the error rate dropped to around 1.5%. Profitability got back on track.

Healthcare Costs

Healthcare is clearly a big decision that affects everybody. The USA spends $7,290 per person on average versus $2,964 among all OECD (Organization for Economic Cooperation and Development) countries. A March 2010 report by Thomson Reuters, a business intelligence service, found that employers' healthcare costs rose 7.3 percent in 2009 compared with 4.8 percent in overall U.S. health spending that year. Small businesses are less likely than large employers to be able to provide health insurance as a benefit. At 12 percent, healthcare is the most expensive benefit paid by U.S. employers, according to the U.S. Chamber of Commerce.

Often healthcare providers themselves struggle with healthcare benefits. One hospital waived the deductible. Employees started to come in for every little medical issue. This created a situation in which it was difficult to see paying patients and put a strain on delivery of service. In addition, because employees were seeking medical attention for everything, the insurance use rate went up — and so did the insurers price for coverage.

These issues came to HR and HR had to take a tough stand for the long term good of the organization. HR had to take a tough stand with insurer and eventually it was financially necessary to change insurers. Changing insurers eliminated going to Hospital for free care. Employees would need to go to in network doctors and make a co-payment.

HR had anticipated push back from employees and so educated them on the cost issues. The hospital would save about a half million dollars annually by changing health care insurers. As it turned out, it was not that big a deal to employees, as they had been uncomfortable going to a colleague for health issues.

Cost of the New Hire Learning Curve

"Hit the ground running." That's what every organization wants from every employee. We can want it; we don't get it. A better idea is to gather data and find out exactly how long it is before an employee can "run." After determining that time, calculate the wages lost during the time the employee is less than 100% productive.

Once you know how much the current ramp up costs, then, look at ways to speed the process. There may be one or several initiatives needed to accelerate the time to 100% productivity. In either case, the kind of data featured below can make the financial case that your initiatives produce a return for the company.

In the example below, based on a $50,000 annual wages employee, the organization lost over $30,000 in wages over a 5 year period. That was for 1 employee. Multiply that by the number of employees hired in that salary range and the losses become staggering. Notice that it takes 27 months, over 2 years, to get the employee up to 80% of productivity. Clearly, initiatives that will bring employees up to speed more quickly will have a financial return.

Months from Hire	3	6	9	12	15	18	21
Productivity	10%	20%	30%	40%	50%	60%	70%
Salary & Payroll Added Costs (PAC)	$5,850	$5,850	$5,850	$5,850	$5,850	$5,850	$5,850
Measure of Productivity	$ 585	1,170	$1,755	$2,340	2,925	$3,510	4,095
Lost Productivity	$5,265	$4,680	$4,095	$3,510	$2,925	$2,340	$1,755

Months from Hire	24	27	30	33	36	39	42
Productivity	75%	80%	85%	90%	91%	92%	93%
Salary & Payroll Added Costs (PAC)	$5,850	5,850	$5,850	$5,851	$5,850	$5,850	$5,850
Measure of Productivity	$4,388	$4,680	$4,973	$,266	$5,324	$5,382	$5,441
Lost Productivity	$1,463	$1,170	$ 878	$ 585	$ 527	$ 468	$ 410

Months from Hire	45	48	51	54	57	60	Lost wages due to learning curve Impact
Productivity	94%	95%	96%	97%	98%	100%	
Salary & Payroll Added Costs (PAC)	$5,850	$5,850	$5,850	$5,850	$5,850	$5,850	
Measure of Productivity	$5,499	$5,558	$5,616	$5,675	$5,733	$5,850	
Loss	$ 351	$ 293	$ 234	$ 176	$ 117	$ -	$ 31,122

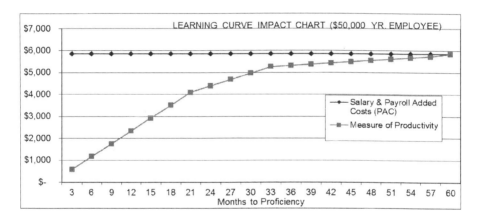

This company analyzed the data and used process improvement methodology to identify and institute several initiatives. These initiatives were designed to achieve 80% productivity 6 months faster. The initiatives included:

- Organized on boarding materials including key organizational contacts, job description, and productivity goals in 3 month increments
- Assigning a mentor to coach the new employee
- Systematizing on-line resources

After instituting the new process, the lost wages was reduced to $23,341, a savings of $7,781 per employee. Clearly the savings here is not the same as a return on investment (ROI) because there is some cost associated with developing and implementing each of the interventions. The ROI would be the savings per employee minus the cost per employee.

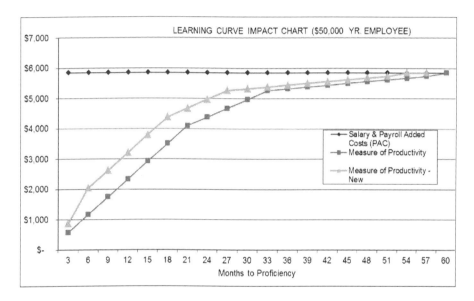

Chapter 7: Answers

Chapter 2 Income and Assets
- ✓ Revenue Trend Data
- ✓ Income Statement

Revenue Trend Data

	Software	Training	Consulting		Total
20xb	$120 M	$ 4 M	$15 M		$139 M
20xa	$110 M	$ 5 M	$12 M		$127 M
20xz	$100 M	$ 5 M	$ 8 M		$113 M
20xy	$100 M	$10 M	$ 8 M		$118 M
20xx	$150 M	$20 M	$10 M		$180 M
Total	$580 M	$49 M	$53 M		$682 M

At first blush it looks as if Software and Consulting are recovering nicely from the economic slump. It also looks as if Training is not recovering as well. Being content with first blush could cause us to miss strategic interventions.

Strategic Investigation

The most strategic thing we can do with those trend numbers is ask questions. Take a moment to look again at the numbers. What questions would you ask about each of the three revenue streams to discover whether HR has a strategic contribution to make?

1. What is the root cause of decreasing training revenue?
2. If training revenues continue to decline what will be corporates strategic response? What can HR do to impact that response?
3. What will it take to get software revenues up to 2006 levels? What role can HR play?
4. How can HR support the consulting function to maintain their revenue increases? If they continue to grow at the current rate, what will change in the division and what will they need from HR?

The answers to your questions will determine HR's strategic involvement.

Income Statement

Strategic Investigation

Take a look at your company's Income Statement, then have a conversation with your friendly, local finance person. What questions will you ask to better understand net income and determine HR's impact it?

1. At a detail level, where are HR related expenses accounted for?
2. What do you include when you talk about "fully loaded" salary costs?
3. Are there any HR items giving you heartburn? What would like to see happen with those items?
4. Where do you anticipate growth in the business? What in your mind will be necessary to support that growth?
5. What are the top 3 concerns/opportunities that HR could address to have the biggest positive impact?

Assets

Strategic Investigation

HR may not have a great deal of impact on tangible assets and yet, HR can have a profound impact on intangible assets. List the ways you impact intangible assets:

1. Branding — How clearly can each person in the organization state the branding message? How willing are they to do it? How vigilant are they in protecting it?
2. Good will — How well do employees serve as organizational ambassadors? How are you positioned in your local community? Are you good corporate citizens?
3. Intellectual Property — How well do employment contracts and non-compete clauses protect the company? What data security processes are in place? How good is the HR partnership with IT on data and knowledge security?
4. Competitive Advantage — How closely do we safeguard our know-how? Our specific combination of skill sets? Our proprietary processes?

One thing HR can impact on the tangible asset side is the need for office space. A well-managed "work from anywhere" process can reduce the need for real estate.

How does your "C Suite" know you have that impact? What evidence do they see?

1. They don't know because we haven't made the case. Ok, time to start connecting the dots between HR initiatives and the specific intangible asset
2. We just agree that HR does the "happy people stuff" and let it go at that. Really? Good luck with that.
3. We do surveys to determine how employees view the organization. A good start on the goodwill side.
4. We review contracts frequently with legal to be sure we protect intellectual property and competitive advantage information.
5. We have processes developed with IT to protect and secure confidential data. We have processes to follow when someone in a sensitive position is let go.

6. We have specific programs and communications to promote brand awareness and brand messaging. We have a media communications protocol in place in the event that a brand is tampered with or found harmful.

It's vital that HR's contribution to intangible assets be clear and recognized. If you were able to easily identify contributions but unable to cite the evidence, there is room for improvement. Consider how you can identify and position the evidence that HR has a positive impact.

Chapter 3 Expenses and Liabilities
✓ Liabilities

Liabilities

Strategic Investigation

What does HR do that has a positive impact on the company's liabilities, that is, use of debt? The concept here is to decrease the need for short and long term debt. Often, analyzing the timing of an initiative can have an impact on the need to borrow.

1. When is the best time to hire? Does a week or a month make a difference in cash flow and a potential need to borrow?
2. If we could negotiate longer payment terms for healthcare benefits, how would that impact cash flow and/or debt?

3. How would electronic payments and electronic deposits (such as salaries) impact cash flow and use of debt?
4. What day of the week or the month is best for making payments?
5. If we use hoteling, can we defer the large debt incurred by renting or buying real estate?

Chapter 4: Tracking money:
✓ Income statement
✓ Balance Sheet
✓ Cash flow statement
✓ Trend Data

Cash Flow Statement

Strategic Investigation

1. Read your company's cash flow statement, in fact read several. Write the questions you have about them that you want to ask your friendly finance person.
2. Help me understand what is included in each category in the cash flow statement?
3. If we looked at several cash flow statements, is our cash flow situation improving, staying the same, getting worse?
4. Where do you see HR having an impact on cash flow?
5. If there were one area where we could have a positive impact on cash flow, what would it be?

6. Are there any troubling trends you see in any of the departments or division?
7. What are your goals for managing cash flow?

Once you have a good understanding of your company's cash flow, analyze the HR initiatives underway. Which of them has a positive impact on cash flow? Which have a negative impact?

HR Initiatives with a positive influence on Cash Flow	Negative Influence:
1. Hiring the right number of people at the right time	1. Increased healthcare costs
2. Supporting process improvement initiatives	2. Increased disability claims
3. Sale force hiring, training, performance	3. Increased insurance prices
4. Reducing paid time off	4. Hiring at the wrong time
5. Increasing productivity; reducing error rates	5. Purchasing at the wrong time

Given your company's financial goals, which initiative would have the greatest positive impact on cash flow? Remember that *reducing* a negative impact can have a positive impact on cash flow. The next step is to run some back of the envelope calculations and talk them over with finance. Finance can help you shape the numbers into a more formal proposal to take to leadership.

Mini Case

Since reducing healthcare costs is an overworked example in the HR profession, let's say you've noticed that the amount paid to contract workers has been on the rise. Contractor expenses are increasing by several thousand dollars every month. Could it be time to hire? Would adding internal position(s) help cash flow by reducing costs?

As a good HR person you reach for the antacids when you learn that technical departments have hired back experts that were laid off last year. Yes, they did hire them back through technical consulting firms but at a premium. Legal issues aside (this is a finance book) is this the most cost effective way to get the work done? Investigation reveals the following:

- Contractor expenses are currently $27,000 per month
- $21,000 went to RentATechie.com
- $11,000 is for your own former employee, a maintenance engineer, $7,000 is for your own former electrical engineer, and $3,000 is for a second electrical engineer.

A conversation with the Operations Manager reveals:
- He'd like to hire one person but the CEO said there was a hiring freeze
- To hire just one person, he'd need a new position with new duties and responsibilities

Identify the numbers/financial information you need to make a **financial** case for hiring rather than continuing to contract:

- Loaded annual salary for the proposed new position
- Total costs of the contractors currently filling the duties of that position

- Length of time to fill the position during which contractors will still be paid
- The financial impact of salary vs. expense paid to the external firm. Salary is a different expense item from payments to vendors. What is the impact of moving from once expense category to another?
- Lost productivity costs of creating the new position plus the cost of the hiring process

Income Statement

Income Statement For PrintPro FY 20xx and 20xy		
	20xx	20xy
Net Sales	$1,500,000	$2,000,000
Cost of Sales	($350,000)	($375,000)
Gross Income	$1,150,000	$1,625,000
Operating Expenses	($235,000)	($260,000)
Operating Income	$915,000	$1,365,000
Other Income (Expense)	$40,000	$60,000
Extraordinary Gain (Loss)	-	($15,000)
Interest Expense	($50,000)	($50,000)
Net Profit Before Taxes (Pretax Income)	$905,000	$1,360,000
Taxes	($300,000)	($475,000)
Net Income	$605,000	$885,000

Mini Case

Based on PrintPro's Income Statements for 2009 and 2010, what conclusions can you draw about the financial health of the company?

1. PrintPro has increased its net income which is generally an indicator of good financial health
2. Net profit has also gone up which is healthy
3. Taxes increased significantly — will this be an issue going forward?

If PrintPro continues the upward trend into the next 2 or 3 years, what can you, the HR Partner anticipate and plan for?

1. Sitting with the senior team to learn the metrics they are using to project growth and to manage costs
2. Determine what balance between increasing productivity of the current workforce and potentially adding personnel will best meet the business metrics.
3. Determining what skill sets will be needed to meet PrintPro's growth needs and determining the most cost effective way to be sure the skill sets are there when needed.
4. Determining where the new business revenues are coming from and developing a plan to support the growth.

Trend Data

Income Statement For PrintPro FY 20xx 20xy and 20xz			
	20xx	*20xy*	*20xz*
Net Sales	$1,250,000	$1,500,000	$2,000,000
Cost of Sales	($345,000)	($350,000)	($375,000)
Gross Income	$905,000	$1,150,000	$1,625,000
Operating Expenses	($230,000)	($235,000)	($260,000)
Operating Income	$675,000	$915,000	$1,365,000
Other Income (Expense)	$20,000	$40,000	$60,000
Extraordinary Gain (Loss)	-	-	($15,000)
Interest Expense	($50,000)	($50,000)	($50,000)
Net Profit Before Taxes (Pretax Income)	$645,000	$905,000	$1,360,000
Taxes	($240,000)	($300,000)	($475,000)
Net Income	$405,000	$605,000	$885,000

Identify the obvious conclusions you can draw from PrintPro's three years of data:

- Net Sales have increased each year.
- Gross Income has increased each year.
- Operating income has increased each year.
- Net Income has increased each year.
- Cost of Sales and Operating Expenses have both gone up each year.

PrintPro's numbers, initially look good. Income numbers are continuously increasing, and it's particularly good that Net Income continues to increase, because that lets us know that expenses, while growing, are not growing disproportionately. Now pull out a calculator. Calculate the following for each year:

- Cost of sales as a percentage of Net Sales each year
- Operating expenses as a percentage of Net Sales each year

	20xx	20xy	20xz
Cost of Sales %	28%	23%	19%
Operating Expenses %	18%	16%	13%

What do those numbers tell you about PrintPro's financial health?

- PrintPro is operating more efficiently as both the Cost of Sales and the Operating Expenses are dropping as a percentage of Net Sales.
- PrintPro is making more money and doing so profitably.

As an HR Partner, what specific initiatives can you undertake/continue that will have a direct financial impact on continuing those financially healthy trends?

- Strategic recognition for those who generated increased sales as well as those who figured out how to operate more cost effectively
- Executive compensation based on the continuation of the current financial trends
- Investigate whether the company can take advantage of any tax breaks related to employment, training, wellness, etc.

Chapter 5 Measures of Profitability:
- ✓ ROE (Return on Equity)
- ✓ ROA (Return on Assets)
- ✓ Time/value of money

Return on Equity

Strategic Investigation

What are the potential relationships of ROE to compensation throughout the organization?

1. The number of people in the organization who can impact ROE is limited to those who make the high level financial decisions. Therefore, compensation or incentives based on ROE don't mean a lot to most people.
2. If incentives are stocks or stock options, then more people might care about ROE, however, most people, even when they own stock, don't necessarily understand how to work toward a stronger ROE

3. ROE may not be the best foundation for incentives because of the above AND because it can be manipulated.

If your executives are incented for achieving a specific ROE how can they virtually guarantee themselves the bonus?

1. Borrow money

Return on Assets

Strategic Investigation:

- Who in your organization would rather receive an incentive based on ROA rather than ROE?

  Operations – they have impact on the ROA
- Who would prefer ROE?

  Finance

Time Value of Money

Mini Case

Your company wants to buy up "Mom and Pop" competitors—let's say HVAC businesses. Your company would first estimate the future cash flows the "Mom and Pop" business would generate, and then discount those cash flows into one lump-sum present value amount, say $750,000. If the owner of the store was willing to sell his business for less than $750,000, the purchasing company would likely accept the offer as it presents a positive NPV investment. Conversely, if the owner will only sell for $750,000 or more, your company wouldn't buy the small business, as the investment would present a negative NPV at that time and would, therefore, reduce the overall value of the company.

- Why should HR care about NPV?

The company being purchased has intangible assets, such as good will, a service ethic, etc. HR can help protect those intangibles by raising the issue of employment agreements, assessing the skill sets of employees and creating a plan to retain the best talent of the company purchased.

- How can HR affect NPV?

Mergers overall tend not to deliver the projected economic value. One of the reasons is that the merging organizations do business differently and productivity is lost in sorting out the two cultures. Involving HR while in negotiation to perform cultural due diligence— that is will the business being purchased be able to maintain or grow during the merger process-- managing the people side of the merger and keeping focus on customer service during and after the merger are important people components that help deliver on the projected NPV.

Clare Novak is an award winning, international facilitator and consultant with over 25 years' experience developing passionate and effective leadership. Focusing leaders on vision, developing positive and respectful relationships and executing on the vision produce bottom line results. Ms. Novak's training and facilitation work optimizes the performance of individuals and teams. She earned her StrengthsFinder® Coaching Certification from Gallup® in 2014.

Ms. Novak's clients range from Fortune 500 to not-for-profit organizations. In addition to the USA, she has worked extensively in Europe, Asia, the Middle East and Africa.

Ms. Novak is the author of *Never Rule Without A Magician, A Sage and A Fool.* She also authored numerous articles, including "Match Made!" *Training & Development Magazine*, "Making the Financial Case for Performance Improvement," *ASTD Info-Line* and "HPI Balanced Scorecard" *ASTD Info-Line*. Clare Novak addressed the ATD International Conference and Expo three times, presented at the SHRM Annual Conference in 2011 and World HRD Congress in 2013.

Clare Novak served on the PA State SHRM Council as Media Relations Director. Previously, she served on the ASTD National Advisors for Chapters, Chaired the Leadership Conference Committee and is a Past President of the Philadelphia ASTD Chapter. She has also served as Professional Development Chair on the Board of Greater Valley Forge Human Resources Association Chapter.

Contact Information

clarenovak@business-leadership-qualities.com

www.business-leadership-qualities.com

https://www.linkedin.com/in/clarenovak

52106720R00067

Made in the USA
Lexington, KY
16 May 2016